13425

AMERICAN COINS AND BILLS

MONEY POWER

Jason Cooper

Rourke

Publishing LLC
Vero Beach, Florida 32964

www.rourkepublishing.com

PHOTO CREDITS: © Armentrout; © Corel Corporation; © Department of the Treasury Bureau of Engraving and Printing; © East Coast Studios; © The Smithsonian Institution National Numismatic Collection; © Lynn M. Stone

Cover Photo: *United States Coins and Bills*

Editor: Frank Sloan

Cover design by Nicola Stratford

Library of Congress Cataloging-in-Publication Data

Cooper, Jason
   American coins and bills / Jason Cooper
      p. cm. — (Money power)
   Includes bibliographical references and index
   Summary: Reveals the history of money in the United States, from the wampum and foreign coins used by colonists, to the new paper money designed to be difficult to counterfeit and the quarters honoring the states.
   ISBN 1-58952-209-5
    1. Money—United States—History—Juvenile literature. [1. Money—United States—History.] I. Title.

HG221.5 .C665 2002
332.4'973—dc21   2001048911

Printed in the USA

TABLE OF CONTENTS

CURRENCY

Currency is another name for paper bills and coins. Currency is used to pay for goods and services. When saved in some form, currency can help people gain **wealth**.

American coins and paper money are made in certain **values** set by the U.S. Government. Canadian coins and bills are made in values set by the Canadian Government.

People use cash registers to keep track of money.

EARLY AMERICAN CURRENCY

America did not become a nation until 1776. Before then, there were 13 colonies under the rule of England. England did not want the colonies making their own money. Still, in 1652, the Massachusetts Bay Colony made its own coins.

American **colonists**, however, largely used goods in place of currency. These goods included furs, grain, and even Indian beads made from shells. These beads were known as **wampum**.

Beads and fur skins were often used as money in early America.

EIGHTEEN PENCE

1/6

No.

EIGHTEEN PENCE,

According to the RESOLVES of the ASSEMBLY of PENNSYLVA-NIA, of the 6th Day of April, in

G   R

the 16th Year of the Reign of His Majesty GEO. the Third. Da-ted at Philadel-phia, the 25th Day of APRIL,

Anno Domini 1776.

1/6

1/6

CONTINENTALS

The colonists did use foreign coins. The foreign coins used most often were Spanish dollars, known as pieces of eight. The Spanish dollar could be nicely cut into eight, pie-shaped pieces to make change.

In 1775 the colonies went to war against England. The new American Government in 1776 began to make paper money to help pay for its war effort. The paper bills were called **continentals**.

THE DEPARTMENT OF
THE TREASURY

In 1789 the U.S. government set up the Department of the Treasury. It was in charge of the first money system. One branch is the Bureau of Engraving and Printing. It made the dollar the basic unit of American money. The U.S. Mint is another branch of the Department of the Treasury. It set up a **mint** in Philadelphia to make coins.

An early dollar bill

U.S. MONEY TODAY

Americans once depended on gold or silver to back the value of their coins and bills. Today the U.S. Government **guarantees** the value printed on a coin or paper bill.

The basic unit of American currency is still the dollar. Each dollar is worth 100 cents. Most American dollars are paper, although some dollar coins are also in use. On each bill are the words, "This note is legal tender…" Legal tender means the dollar must be accepted as payment for goods and services in the United States.

New designs on bills were issued beginning in the 1990s.

NUMBERS ON MONEY

Numbers are used on all United States currency. The numbers on a coin show its value and the year it was minted. The large number printed on the corners of the front side of a bill shows its value. A serial number on each bill gives it a special identity. A bill also shows the year it was printed.

The value of these bills is shown by the numbers printed in the corners.

Schools need money to buy computers and supplies.

Beginning in 1999, new quarters that honored the 50 states were issued.

WORDS ON CURRENCY

American currency includes several words along with the numbers. The term "United States of America" appears on all currency along with the value, such as "Ten Dollars."

"Liberty," because of its importance to Americans, appears on all coins. "In God We Trust" appears on all American currency minted or printed since 1984.

Other words identify people and places shown on currency. The Latin words *E pluribus unum* mean "Out of many, one." These words appear on most coins.

Along with words, American money also has pictures. George Washington's picture is on the dollar bill and quarter.

FRONT AND BACK

The front side of U.S. currency has a picture of a famous American. The secretary of the U.S. Treasury chooses the picture. It cannot be of a living person. With a few exceptions, pictures on American currency honor past presidents.

The back side of currency usually shows a historic place. The Lincoln Memorial, for example, is on the back of a $5 bill.

1. Front and back of penny
2. Front and back of nickel
3. Front and back of dime
4. Front and back of quarter

1

2

3

4

CHANGING AMERICAN CURRENCY

U.S. paper money is printed in values of 1, 2, 5, 10, 20, 50, and 100 dollars. Until 1969 $5,000 and $10,000 bills were printed.

Money designs change, too. In the late 1990s, bills were printed in a new style. To date, only the 1 and 2 dollar bills have not been changed. These changes made it more difficult for **counterfeiters** to copy the bills.

In 1999 the U.S. Treasury began to mint a series of new quarters to honor each of the 50 states. The quarters are being released at the rate of five states per year through 2008.

GLOSSARY

colonists (KAHL uh nists) — the people from Europe who in 17th century America started the settlements called colonies

continentals (KAHN teh NEN tulz) — the first paper money bills issued by the Continental Congress of 18th century America

counterfeiters (KOUN tur FIT uhrz) — people who make fake money

currency (KER en see) — money, especially paper money

guarantees (gayr un TEEZ) — backs up the value of money

mint (MINT) — a place where coins are made; to make, or manufacture, coins

values (VAL yooz) — the amount of money something is worth, or that people will pay for it

wampum (WAHM pum) — beads or polished shells used by North American Indians as money

wealth (WELTH) — any type of property with value in money; a gathering of properties

INDEX

Further Reading

Abeyta, Jennifer. *Coins*. Children's Press, 2000
Bressett, Kenneth (Ed.) and Yeoman, Richard. *A Guide Book of U.S. Coins*.
    St. Martin's Press, 2000

Websites To Visit

http://www.treas.gov/opc/
http://www.frbsf.org/currency/index.html
http://www.moneyfactory.com

About The Author

Jason Cooper has written several children's books about a variety of topics for Rourke Publishing, including recent series *China Discovery* and *American Landmarks*. Cooper travels widely to gather information for his books. Two of his favorite travel destinations are Alaska and the Far East.